*Gentle Northern Summer*

# Gentle Northern Summer

### GEORGE STANLEY

New Star Books
Vancouver
1995

*For my poetry buddies, James Liddy & Barry McKinnon*

Published by New Star Books Ltd., 2504 York Avenue, Vancouver, B.C.
V6K 1E3. All rights reserved. No part of this work may be reproduced or
used in any form or by any means — graphic, electronic, or mechanical —
without prior permission of New Star Books. Any request for photo-
copying or other reprographic copying must be sent in writing to the
Canadian Copyright Licensing Agency (CANCOPY), 900 - 6 Adelaide
Street East, Toronto, Ontario M5C 1H6.

The lines from Margaret Avison's *No Time* are reprinted with the
permission of Margaret Avison and Lancelot Press.

Cover art by Nhan Duc Nguyen
Cover designed by Val Speidel
Printed and bound in Canada by Best Book Manufacturers
1 2 3 4 5  99 98 97 96 95

Publication of this book is made possible by grants from the Canada
Council and the Cultural Services Branch, Province of British Columbia

**Canadian Cataloguing in Publication Data**

Stanley, George
  Gentle northern summer

  Poems.
  ISBN 0-921586-54-X

I. Title.
PS8587.T36G4  1995     C811'.54     C95-910764-9
PR9199.3.S72G4  1995

# Contents

NEW POEMS 1992-94

*Gentle Northern Summer*

# Gentle Northern Summer

## 1

Looking out window at neighbour's spread,
vast spaces 'bourgies' think they deserve ...

(Why judge? What do I care?)

Later, on the grass:

Gentle northern summer, do I face
my uncaringness when my mind
is filled with you? In this gentle time
of trees & bees & clover feel a wordless
reprobation to discover

behind their placid faces & doors
a secret that unites them, willy-nilly,
with the coal trains coming, five years
'down the road'?

(coal dust on leaf & air, in
nostril & ear, 500-mile-long smudge)

(A mile from the tracks you don't
notice the whistle, in the buzz & hum
of insects & reliable appliances

(Nor 4,000 miles east do New York bankers
coming out the glass doors of their Park Avenue
ziggurats see any coal dust either
in the edited texture of events their eyes
pick up

(30 km south my neighbour, F's, pickup
crosses the red cantilever bridge
over the Kitimat River & speeds up the hill
& as he makes the turn at the top, he takes in
the view, of the Kitimat Valley, mountains & mist,
    splendid —
takes it home with him, in fact, it's part of his
lifestyle
            but the clearcuts that hang over us
(like swaths made by the teeth of aliens)
are not part of the 'views' we appropriate,
they are external
                    the scraped
slopes evidence value
racked up somewhere, some
big account
            *Haul it out,*
*& then we'll go mining.* And the ranch houses
stay put, tame trees on the lawn,
on the crimeless streets

**2**

*for Daniel*

At a table in the old Houston hotel:

'Each time,' Vivian said,
'people got moved out of the way,
Indians, then farmers, then came the mill
& mine, & now (swinging her arm wildly) that mall,
that none of them know what's happening to them.'

('The real Trojan horse,' Spicer wrote,
'was Greek sentence structure. The Trojans
never knew what hit them.')

*People of this north will have to change
their ways* (some newspaper)

      Who counts
the changes? a child growing up
in Houston, say, to Indians, bear & moose

(swimming across the river to the hippie houses
& their eyes told / what had moved them)

to teenage void & foreseeing heavy industry
knocking the moly out of the mountains
(not Homer's herb / that kept men sane,
protected from being turned to pigs,
but silver grit that hardens steel for war
to see who will control these malls, these stalls

He sees the bland & bowed consumer heads
in Ali Baba's cave, pass the tumbled piles
of glittery cloth, cold sparkle of death games,
pink Mexican fruit,
their eyes all inward turned
on private catalogues

At the checkout stand he sees
the illusion & the cash
change hands (with thank you on both sides).
The former goes eventually to the dump
(of things that cease to charm),
the cash goes to Vancouver
(by computer),
             & sees, *we* are the natural
resources, that 'mix our hands with the earth'
& drive from mill to mall to spend our pay —
the suckers at the breast of dreams

If all this were brought down
quite suddenly, he'd say
people'd rise up in anger
(but with no world to compare it to?)

(& it done slickly, equipment
moved on site, oiled, the go-ahead
archival by the time the wheels turn)

(& if they dare,
the system, the tangled boundary
(that has no place in what we learn as place)
deflates, at every encountered point
draws back with a gasp at being
unappreciated, dangles some plastic
goodies in our faces, some go-cart

& we go off gaily in the snow
follow the moose droppings

then it swells up again, aggrieved
but deferent, gets to work, pumping

value


### 3

Looking out the window I can see
nothing of the life I'm buried in,
slippage, moraine —

The ranch houses
like a row of broken columns,
tame trees on the lawn. Behind them,
the half-wild second growth in their hundreds,
hemmed in by the bench. More houses,
in the air, some for sale.
It is so still & dreamlike.

To get one more tankful of gas,
I drive to the pump.
Like my neighbour, I accede
to the coal trains coming,
the rearming of Japan, whatever.

The secret is not in the picture.
It is in some closeup of our lives
that we cannot see, smeared over us
like a recurring decimal.

## 'The world is the case'

This point in putting together
a picture puzzle,
   when you've almost got the border
complete, & pieces of faces
& roads are becoming recognizable,
masses of foliage, lanterns,

that your heart begins to sicken
of it (just the point when
   each gap closed
yields maximum information)
is what it's like, here
or elsewhere.

# My New Past

*for Daniel Ignas*

'I can go back to my old past whenever I
want, to times in my childhood, or college.
But my new past never happened.'
                                    *Joy, at the Achillion*


Did we spend four years — a high school
or college length of time — when every week,
once, twice or several days, sometimes
whole days together, we met, hung out, talked,
touched (in that poor-spiritual way
men have), & not a trace of it all
left?

        Not true: certain eternal
moments survive; the first one, for example:
your Panama hat, Lawrence's horse. But each
is a 'treasured memory,' a mental
vignette. The place they were
is gone. Where is North Central B.C.,
August, 1982, at this hour?

Further & further on, but less & less
tied to what went before,
I seem to be journeying. The image is
sand. Peripherally haunted by its
random sculpture, unmoving but shifted

under changing skies. Every morning
I wake to a blank, then deduce
the separation. I used to go,
*1968, 1970, 1971, 1974, 1976* —
private hopscotch, contrived
for the player's solace.

                   My new past
never happened, is not available
for edification. Nor is the present
a distillate. There is some other
kind of causality than history. To take
a catchphrase from the airlines, a
hub-spoke arrangement, each year
a separate outpost of childhood,
no advance.

             And maturity
is getting used
to this scattered country. Who told us
we would cross the River of Lethe
in this life?

            Wordsworth and Eliot,
when they got here, & saw they had
no baggage, smiled, & wrapped their loss
in forgiveness.

            Forgiveness of whom?
The child I was, not knowing life would come
to sand & snow? Or my new self, drifted,
encamped, below the mountains.

# Terrace '87

High snow on rock a word

I sit in my campchair, aware

Distance is false, all is here
in the sky

Then giant cracks
break the summer air,
courtesy Kitimat Chamber of Commerce

I hear Nechako raindrops falling
inside a mountain,
river torn from valley,
chained, head down, in a tunnel

drives turbines
till pure inanimate power shines forth.

(I see the Alcan shareholder smile,
slitting open his broker's statement.)

At the Inn of the West
(some still call the Lakelse)
the Terrace Chamber, in fern-filled
morning sunlight, dreams:

'energy-intensive industries' —
technology, an elixir —

jobs for 'the youth'
(remembering when they last felt young
sales were up, there was a kid
to boss around the store) — Capital

(Dudley Little said it years ago:
'Without Columbia [Cellulose]
[now Westar] we'd be nothing')

grant us our lifestyle.

         •

I see now the young Nisga'a, heir
to skinned hills, rotting stumps
(Tree Farm Licence One)
dance backwards into Greig Avenue
away from the enraged 'white man'
with the pool cue
                & I think
he's a raindrop
skipping over the land
until he splashes

         •

& settler boys
not talking, stand
in sapling clumps
with rockstar hair

or roll along the avenue
on big wheels & cutout pipes
going somewhere
(going where the pavement goes,
to the corner)

trained
      to want.

        •

The mill or smelter
a shiny device
to the eyes of Rotary
(on its long coffee break)

Boys go in,
workers come out
with credit cards — neat!

(but it's Sam Clark's mill,
it doesn't need any workers,
it doesn't even have any floors,
it's self-lubricating
(maybe just the occasional polishing rag)

        •

ALL WE WANTED
WAS A FREE RIDE
Is that too much to ask?

All we wanted
was that moment
when you pass

& the other guy's face
is blank
behind glass

Then the blank guy
wants to pass

●

And if the fish flop,
spawning,
on Nechako gravel beds . . .

(José plays a lot of Liszt
lately.)

There are no words for the fish
the Indians said
shared their lives
with us.
Our food comes by truck.

The boys laugh: Maybe
we'll have to fight for this land.
(& their dads think: tourism.

(& their dads think:
the kids don't want to work anyway,
it's what they teach them. Big corporations
have all the money anyway. Let them
create the jobs.

●

Fall. The rainstorm chutes
long logs down the slopes, jams
the culvert, caves the road. Tractor-trailers
stack up. Our food, our body, our lifestyle.

●

December. Coloured lights sketch
houses of family. Arms control descends
like a gift of Titans. Like little pre-Christian men

imagined Thor, or Russian serfs
a good Tsar. Up where satellites crawl,
Star Wars lasers, power'd by earth's rivers, may streak.
Today benevolence speaks, sublunary commanders

& we've never been so far from the stars,
that were our friends.

# San Francisco's Gone

*for Gerald, much love*

*and in memory*
*of Edward Dermott 'Ned' Doyle*
*who taught me poetry*
*and gave me reasons to travel*
*north of California St.*

## 1

For a fraction of a second behind tired eyes
image of SF waterfront circa 1950
from deck of SP ferry
                    emerging from beneath
double-deck Bay Bridge; splayed piers flank
Arthur Paige Brown's Ferry Building,
'20s skyscrapers, Russ & the phone company,
& the nozzle atop Telegraph Hill, in scale
with the human houses, high-ceilinged neighborhoods,
ascending steep slopes of bluebrown Twin Peaks.

All night drinking on the train
from Stockton: USF football game,
Dons beat COP 56-7 (?)
    — the train must have been shunted over Western Pacific
    tracks — I think we passed through Tracy — or held on
    sidings, to take all night to get from Stockton to Oakland
    (80 miles?)

I started drinking beer that summer, with Tom Gallagher,
Bert Schaefer, and Neil Battaglia, in Tom's car, parked
somewhere out in the Sunset with the lights out, a
weekday night, cold quarts of Burgie or Regal Pale
in paper bags

In June I'd graduated from SI, walked up the center aisle of
St. Ignatius twice — once for the Martin Latin medal and
once for the scholarship to USF — then last, in alpha-
betical order, to accept the ribbon-tied scroll from the
priest sitting in a carved armchair below the altar (my
rival, LaForest 'Frosty' Phillips, beat me though; he went
up for three prizes)

I was a sissy in high school, & got picked on a lot, & so,
started hanging out with these older guys, Tom, Bert, and
Neil (whom I'd impressed with my wits, I could make
them laugh), I'd met working as a page after school at the
Main Library (McAllister & Larkin, architect George
Kelham, 1917 (?)), & drinking beer (so maybe it was
earlier than that summer)

Drank vodka (in a bag) for the first time at a college 'smoker'
& woke up the next morning in the back seat of some-
body's convertible, splattered with the necessary dried
vomit, the car being parked not on any street but askew in
the parking lot at the center of campus, many students at
10 o'clock class break peeking in the window

& became a football fan. That year the Dons went
undefeated, so, traveled on the chartered fans' train to
Stockton to see them whomp COP. Next Monday USF
was ranked 10th in the UPI coaches' poll. 1951, Ollie
Matson's year.

San Francisco, as it looked then.


2

*Her first day at the office*
*all lunch hour she walked round the block*
*too shy to go in a restaurant*

One of several times I visited my Aunt Catherine, my
    mother's younger sister, a nun in her seventies, at the
    convent in San Jose, she told this story. We were sitting
    in the sunny visitors' parlor, on spotless upholstered
    furniture, that had been my mother's.

If she went to work at 17, that would have been 1921
    or 2. I imagine the building as Kelham's Standard Oil of
    California headquarters at Bush & Sansome (that went up
    in '21). After her dad lost his coal & wood yard in Daly
    City (gas now cheap enough for cooking), she had to go
    to work. Big corporations were hiring women for office
    work — SP, Standard Oil, PG&E (that sold the gas).
    Catherine would have been 13.

California corporations put up neo-Gothic skyscrapers (25
    stories, tops) on landfill placed in the '70s over the wrecks
    of sailing ships (the original waterfront was just east of
    Montgomery)

I imagine the block she walked around as Bush Montgomery
    Pine Sansome, every building new or under construction,
    bare steel & the flash & sputter of oxy-welding,
    excavations, wagons, horses, men: a boom built on fire
    insurance proceeds (five Eastern companies bankrupted)
    & loans from the new Bank of America (backed by grain
    & fruit receipts)

Jack had come out from Cork in the '90s. (His cousins in
   Menlo Park who had emigrated earlier thought of Jack
   (and Mamie, whose father Michael was a day laborer) as
   'Irish,' but considered themselves 'Californians' (this is
   also Catherine's memory).) When he lost his business he
   went to work for C&H Sugar, the Hawaiian growers'
   refinery in Crockett. Boarded, came home weekends &
   Christmas. The gold 25-year pin with diamond chip,
   which he received on retirement (and which was sent to
   me after Catherine's death, in 1985, by the Sisters) reads:
   *J. Hennessy 4-16-41.*

25 years a farm boy in Cork, 25 or so an Irish-Californian
   worker, then merchant, then at 50 a sugar worker. Mamie
   and the four children moved back downtown, to a flat in
   an alley off 15th & Church. Marie would have taken the
   'J', or one of the Market cars, to work. Mamie (or Mary, as
   she wrote on job applications) went to work for the SP,
   when Catherine and Francis were older.

*For it was Mary, Mary*
*long before the fashion came*

Marie, a French name, why? A cachet
of elegance, before the Fire?

*Though with propriety, society*
*would say Ma-rie*

And the shyness, of the Catholic girl,
near country girl, grew up on a kind of farm
next to a coal & wood yard

Brown hair, fair skin, freckled.
Hazel eyes. *Petite*, five-one.

Learned her Palmer hand
at Mission Dolores, typing
at the office. Early as I can remember,

the grocery list with one or two items
neatly crossed out. She could balance her checkbook.

### 3

The first-born, her brother Emmett,
graduate of Sacred Heart, attending
night law school at St. Ignatius, working days
on the front desk at the St. Francis: their hope.

Imagine a weekend excursion to Santa Cruz.
The SP train leaves from 3rd & Townsend.
Emmett, his sister Marie, his girl friend Regina,
his friend George Stanley from the hotel.
Cousin Mary gets on at Menlo. They take

a couple of cabins in a tourist court
near the beach. Do they bring
blankets from the City or borrow the ones in the cabin
to spread on the sand? The striped
beach umbrella goes up, the girls in one-piece
suits (& caps if they go in), the men
in baggy trunks run in the surf, their feet
slap the wet sand, they bat
the beach ball. Big green waves
off Monterey Bay break.

In the evening
they walk the boardwalk, or 'invest'
a dime in the player piano with seven
percussion instruments banging in the Casino.
Throw the baseball, knock over the milk bottles.
The booth lights glance in the soft waves
of the girls' hair.

& back at the cabin play swing records
on the wind-up Victrola (I guess),
& later in the decade
mix orange blossoms: canned juice
& bathtub gin. Young, happy
white collar workers

Happy to return to the City


4

George (there was a photograph, part of his face
    in slanting shadow, the mouth obscure)
was in the Navy,

was out in the Atlantic once, on a destroyer but
    not far, nowhere near the U-boats
(the war — for improvement — like the Panama Canal)

At Pelham Bay Naval Station, New York, he had 'flu.
Discharged in '19, sailed for home, & to return

to his widowed father, George Albert Stanley, civil
    engineer
and Grand Secretary of the Young Men's Institute (the
    Catholic 'Y'), club & baths at 50 Oak St.,

living in an apartment on Turk, or Octavia . . . check
   the city directory.

The ex-sailor was George *Anthony* Stanley,
the friar patron of lost belongings exchanged
for the Prince Consort. And that was his mother,
Molly McCormick's, gift.

Did Marie tell me he wrote poetry? Or that, enroute,
   he stayed, several days, a sojourn
(or was it just a shore visit, a few hours?)
in Havana, Cuba, & thought of not
coming back, but going on to Brazil?

because that's where I imagine him, a serious —
   *a dreamy*, dark, narrow-headed boy,
      with stiff black hair. I see him at a table (marble top)
      in a sidewalk cafe, or walking the Malecon
      into a summer wind, but can't imagine how he imagined

that break, what image, song, or deeper will
called him —
                     but instead returned

to the Grand Secretary, who lives at the William Taylor
   Hotel on McAllister, & takes all his meals out now,
   accompanied by his boy,

and a job on the front desk at the St. Francis.

Emmett invites him up to his mother's place, at 11 Carl.
In the front room Ma plays the upright, a
vigorous bass, bright treble, plinking
above high C, rippling streams.

Then the girls gather round chorusing,
'Come, Josephine, In My Flying Machine'

& the men, in good clothes, seated
on Mamie's mahogany furniture, served
cake & claret.


                    5

They were good houses, built by small contractors
    working out of sheds in alleys, mixing concrete &
    pouring foundations, blueprints on site. On the
    side streets —
Clayton, Shrader — wider types of Queen Anne Victorian —
    big, gabled attics, broad sidewalks for play. On
    Carl
(the arterial, later the car-line) older, narrower styles,
    flat roofs. The Haight
is forty years or so old, in '33. Sunny Jim had been Mayor,
now Governor. You repainted your house every five years,
    you & your brother-in-law. Borrow the ladder. With
    a hoist you could tar your own roof.

Now down the north side of Haight of a Spring morning
    comes Mrs. Murphy, a fat (not stout) French (Franco-
    American?) lady, in black (like the other morning
    shoppers) — black straw hat, black purse, & in the purse
    the worn leather change purse; from the Superba, crossing
    at Cole, in front of the stopped Haight cars, wagons &
    trucks, to Romey's, to get canteloupe or celery 3¢ cheaper.
    Her new downstairs tenant, Marie Stanley, often
    accompanies her, but not today, she ran up Carl
    to her mother's place, number 11.

The front parlor of Ma's upstairs flat (Marie walks down the
    hall) is silent, as is the back dining room. Jack is in
    Crockett. Marie sits at the kitchen table. Ma comes up the
    back stairs with marigolds, picked from slat-bordered beds
    in the backyard. Pokes the fire in the grate, moves some
    stewing apples away from the heat, pours coffee. She sits
    down across from Marie, who tells her hesitant secrets.

Sunlight sparkles in the high windows; outside, clothes on
    the line wave, trees in other yards. The bride & the bride's
    mother talk, of the new husband and the old one, the one
    away, the father. The things to be done for the men who
    come home.

(When I saw the bride's face at Carew & English
not looking upward from the satin,
I saw by the line of her jaw it was my grandmother's,
previously concealed by amiable laughter)


### 6

& George went to the PG&E for a year —
on the metal monster, through the new Sunset Tunnel —

then the Hall, with its green-patina'd dome
    (was it gilt in '15?), Arthur Brown, Jr.'s
couchant sphinx-headquarters, with wings for legs
    (when whizbangs flew & mustard gas crept
at Ypres), colonnaded tribute to Sunny Jim Rolph's
    honest administration, and symbol
of the new City risen from the ashes, after

years of graft, trials of the Board of Supervisors,
Boss Ruef's creatures, interrupted by the Fire,
    was to be

the major effect in Daniel Burnham's 'City Beautiful'
    plan, if hungry businessmen had not
sunk that dream (hardly vision), gone back to
    making money on the
old plat, stacking the bricks the morning after
the Fire
            (and well they did, can you imagine the City's hills
draped in landscaped avenues, like ramps on the contours?)

    The Fire that George remembers (he was eight,
walked with his father to the north/south ridge of the City,
    Laurel Hill cemetery (they were living somewhere out
on Turk), walked with thousands up to the Park, there
    they turned around, looked east.
On that April day, winds blew. Sky was red. 50,000 people
    stood & watched
the red sky, & then the red & black sky, & heard
    all day & all night, the roar
of the flames, & the falling of buildings.

& on the weekend, smart guys neatly stacked the bricks
(but who could, Bean says somewhere, tell the lessees
    from the looters?)


                    7

Late afternoon. Fog comes, in gusts, streamers,
then a damp wall over the Park. The custard-white
spires of St. Ignatius shine bright above. Like bishops.

Sand is still blowing in the Sunset, houses
hammered in the sand dunes, boys climbing in the unbuilt.

## 8   UNDER THE DOME

A 12′ oak-paneled office, upper walls off-white.
Black tabulating & card-sorting machines. The boy sits
at an unused desk, randomly fingering the keys
of a comptometer. The man turns

from the women in black smocks with white
lace collars (who turn too), a white card
in a black wood frame, held out,
a word in black caps, glassed:

THINK

IBM

Then down the marble corridor
of the north wing to a second office.
Women looked up from their typing,
they worked for him, as he worked
for Mr. Brooks, & Tom Brooks worked for Mayor Rossi.
     Part of the dome is seen,
chalk-green, in a window above him.

FDR was President, Pius XII Pope, Joe Louis
heavyweight champion. We were winning the war,
a sure thing, but he, though complacent
as any Democrat, disliked the routine.
He knew the City was built on sand and an
underground river, that they pumped
water out of the Opera House basement
     24 hrs. a day.

What was in front of
my face when he held out
that card in its black frame
but his body, white shirt, Paisley tie
hanging, belt & buckle. (The card lay
in the top drawer of the highboy years,
    under socks.)

When he threw me in the ocean
I can't even remember yelling,
only running back up the sand
to the umbrella, remains of picnic lunch.
Ocean Beach. (The sand was dirtier now,
there were things in it. Bottle caps.)

In his office he tried to show the boy
the trustworthiness of the City, souls
shaped by official duties.
He couldn't believe it.
So we went back to water.

In the clammy indoor pool
of the YMI, the boy
willed his body to sink, would not
be buoyant.

        Of what
importance is it except to do
justice to the pain of his want,
his lack, holding out a gift that was not
his to give, his version of manhood, boyhood.
He was not a giver. He was a poet,
    a sailor,

manqué. The boy rejected
the mirage projected
from some beyond
& bounced off Ireland.

We stood naked in the shower room
& his will backfired on his eye,
his secret passion stole the boy away
on waves of adventure, & in that moment,
   his lostness
was the true gift.


### 9

Once, on the streetcar, the 'L', going downtown,
a sunny Saturday, maybe the fall of '47,
him 48, me 13, heads bent, an intense
conversation, in the dark, varnished seats
at the back of the car. It had begun

even before we sat down, taking transfers
from the conductor (were we going
to the ball game?) I could tell
he wanted out, that he looked towards San Diego
(we had spent a couple of weeks there, that summer)

as he had to Brazil. There were breezes & shadows,
the metal monster rolled smoothly along Market
from Castro to Sanchez. He had a grey hat on
with the snap brim turned up
all around. We wore thin McGregor jackets,
grey or beige. We were almost friends.

He told me what it meant to be
George Stanley, with only wit as a plea.

He tried to pass on to me
the name, Anthony, his mother had found
to replace the alien Albert. He wanted me

to be Tony, it fit the land, he said, like Mission
architecture, women liked it. I could not
take that talisman, happiness, from him.
Loyally I chose to continue his fuckup.


### 10

Ten years later he comes home on the 'L',
the pink *Call-Bulletin* folded under his arm,
takes off his hat, in the kitchen
lifts his glass of Roma port to her, tells her
(again) how he hates the place,
the Hall. The leisurely civil service manner
adopted by Blacks or Samoans seems to him
misconduct.


### 11  ISLANDS

> All the islands swam across the Atlantic
> and became parishes in New York.
>
> *James Liddy*

But James, some of them must have swum
further, by Panama portage come to a Golden Gate,
a Catholic country whose cathedral debt was paid
by transcontinental train time ('69).

                          Shanty Irish
south o' the slot, & lace curtain Irish
sticking flowers in vases to place on tables
even when there was nobody dead.

Tobins
of the Hibernia sucked deposits to the
heights (like, Ashbury?), & lent them out
past the panic of '73 when even Ralston
(of the Bank of California, he who had planted
eucalyptus seeds in the Panhandle) jumped in the Bay;

small factories, one or two story buildings,
iron workers, brass founders, flour millers,
stitching bags to fill, wagons to carry
     cross town,
living in flats over stores, yet building,
out Mission & Howard & Folsom (where Mission makes
the big bend towards Spain), *palaces* . . .

'copies of fragments of palaces . . . thin, wooden, box-like
     structures with bay windows,' thus Arthur Paige
     Brown's scorn for the people's
mansions, Victorians he saw first in the '80s,
brown-wallpapered, tintype-laden, gas-lit,
that packed the 11th ward, & pushed out

towards Daly City, farms.

Small families. Not because of safes
but diphtheria. To their priceless
children, nuns spoke
blandly of Hell, at the bottom of space,
with its tortures,
                    & even in the public
schools, teachers said, 'absolution,'
faced down nativist rage.

The islands: St. Joseph's, St. Rose's, St. Peter's.
St. John the Baptist, on Eddy. St. Agnes
(of the Haight). St. Anne of the Sunset.


## 12   THE WHITE CLIFFS OF DOELGER

Henry J., developer, when land was free
& work was cheap (& the 17 car 5 cents)
financed and oversaw the building of
good houses in long, north-south blocks

on the Parkside slope. Retained damp sand
by concrete wall, water pipes
the City put in, big creosoted redwood poles,
crossarm'd, upheld the wires (as they still do).

Each bungalow, stucco'd, painted white (a few
pink, yellow, green — the colors of frosted cakes)
looked down blacktop streets with white lines

to the Pacific. And the ocean breathed its condensation back
high as Twin Peaks over my head
all spring & early summer, morning's womb.


## 13

From the earliest she dwelt in Heaven, its brown,
     sloping hills,
that California bruited as an afterlife
for suffering Ireland. Gossoons,
unmarried at 40, made their way here,
stepped stiffly from the train at Oakland Pier,
bachelor uncles needing to be cooked for.

These were the duties of the daughter, to turn
the profusion of Paradise into family meals.
The gas range saved her labor but demanded
by its white enamel hauteur more devotion
(& kneeling polishing Mondrian linoleum)
than her mother's wood floors & coal hod
& lump coal in dusty bags leaning by the pantry.

Then needed a green car to drive her mother
to doctors. The young men of the good time still wearing
collar & tie toed it to the Park from the rest home run by
'that woman' to whom she wrote checks.

She was on *some other work*, her clothing,
serviceable coats, hats with perfunctory veil,
showed it: determination & later hair color.
She wore flowers like they were ornaments.

In the bath she would wash my hair, then rub it dry,
brisk, detached. The phone would ring during dinner.

And kept all the accounts. Angel of mercy
arriving on time, Hayward or Hayes St.
    Later schoolchildren
knew her reliability, her love.

In the hospital, on Darvon, she patted her thigh
where the cancer grew & said, 'My friend.'


### 14

After her death, George & George & Gerald
walking up Taraval from the Riviera Restaurant
(not North Beach of the '50s, but credible Italian food,
water & a basket of bread on the table before ordering),

Dad walked away into the shade of a building
to pee. So there we were, like we didn't need
facilities. No longer separate in time, but in fact
friends, boys, three sons of a dead saint.

## 15 HER DREAM

In the Sunset, in the '50s, her soul breathes easy.
She walks to the retail, noting with approval
disappearance of vacant lots, sand & iceplant,
houses & stores going up, even without lawns,
flush with the sidewalk; & from her back window sees
terraced houses, white blocks,
covering up the dunes, leaving only
a strip of beach: families moving
in, taming finally this almost empty
Spanish shore, home to seagulls, a sense
of reward for rightness.

                Now there's happiness,
a living room furnished from the Emporium,
rose brocade drapes, gold sofa & chairs,
tables, & friends make up a club, a parish
salary-rich, a new church, bell
tower & baldacchino (fixed canopy over the altar)
rises from the striped parking lot
(Archbishop Mitty charged the going rate on the loan).

The City is built now, it stays poised
here for a moment, respectable,
inviting speculation, till a generation
dies or moves down the Peninsula.

Marie has the club over
after Christmas midnight mass.

A police lieutenant, the vice-president
of Cal-Pak, big men in blue suits,
gripping highballs, stand in her living room
(& George stands among them, in white shirt & tie,
    but not quite
of them, something odd about him, McGinty, the VP,
    has said,
not unkindly, mind somewhere else.

                              Marie bustles
among the men & their wives, with hors d'oeuvres.
The blue & silver balls gleam on the artificial tree
& Crosby sings on the hi-fi, 'Adeste . . . '

After they leave something takes her back.
A holy card in her missal. Her thoughts go back
to the Mission, she sees again
the crowded streets, where it all went on
in flesh and blood. Streetcars clanged,
priests hurried past, to the sick,
her aunts dressed in black for shopping,
butcher on 16th St. with the sawdust
& pink butcher paper — living world —
& all seemed to know it was one —
bread meat fur flowers —
moves her heart, not Paradise
but plain reality lost.

Illusion, I want to tell her.
Like the Milky Way, the galaxy seen
through its longest dimension, packed with stars.

I want to tell her the stars walk alone.

Time packs truths closer, events flock on
   hills of knowledge
(& she nods & smiles, dreaming alone)

Her truth now wakes in my mind
& where there was bleakness or a gash in meaning

(George & George & Gerald sat in the coffee shop
on Polk St., a block down from the hospital,
commenting lamely on the service, the waitress, even
half-heartedly joking, for each other, then in silence
turned back to her again, her worn, sweet face — she
loved — it doesn't matter who

We can part, Marie & I,
if we can each remember
a mother whose eyes showed care,
the home look

Sometimes, a heart waits
unable to answer, or do more than
look from the window,
fondly, unseen

Marie, who bore me.

# San Jose Poem

for Catherine Hennessy
(Sister Maureen) (1908-85)

Starting in April, sadness
carried forward from Catherine's death
which I have not mourned, in April,
in April sadness

how the city of San Jose stands in my mind,
the B of A with its bell-less tower,
hot 5 p.m., walking east on Santa Clara
cross Market and First

preserved façades,
south between Second and Third
sun on car roofs, blocks
razed to keep Mexicans from crossing
(some stores left hang
banners in Vietnamese)

South of Keyes
were orchards

•

       Sunday afternoons
we drove to orchards

a grey DeSoto
or Dodge sedan, moving slowly down

gravel roads
quarter-sections of trees
geometrically spaced,
watered

the grey Coast hills
beyond

Visitors, we parked
in front of a small barn,
were allowed to walk in among the trees,
reached into our hands & mouths
Santa Clara plums, a sweet
green fig, ripe apricots.
Our friends gave us balsa cartons
to take fruit back to the City.

•

Catherine came
to San Jose as Superior
of the convent, her last assignment.
12 years she had been Superior of the Order.

At her funeral mass Gerald said
(in his homily)
she was not one of the foolish virgins
nor would she have been one of the 'sensible' virgins
either, refusing oil to her foolish sisters,
telling them to go downtown and buy some

She would have been in the Lord's house already
placing a glass of gingerale and a cookie
in the room of each one arriving home late

as she came to the side door
of the Hayes St. convent in San Francisco
with wax-paper sandwiches
of cabbage & mashed potato
for men who lined up
in the Depression.

·

Catherine entered the Sisters
of the Holy Family in 1930.
The order, since 1872,
patronized by Irish banks, established
day homes, for children of
poor: in San Jose,
cannery workers.

The fruit
left by train. The trees
sucked the water out of the ground
& it left as fruit. Water in a well
(Santa Clara & Delmas)
150 ft. (1950).

The sisters lived in underheated
California baroque luxury (mahogany paneling).

Sr. Thomasine held me as a child.

Last year, Sr. Daniel, her sister, served
shrimp salads, steaks, rolls, ice cream & coffee
to Catherine & me
in the Superior's dining room.

These people are still alive
& live on St. Elizabeth's Drive

in San Jose (& they are dead & live in this poem
with the often repetitive movements of the dead,
drawing in a skirt, just so, as to be remembered
in rooms filled with spring sunlight
& my mother's spotless furniture.

●

Leaving the convent, dazed, dazzled
by goodness I'd go back to the Holiday Inn
generously contemptuous of the ones who ate avocado
salads in the Hawaiian coffee shop or played
video games in the black alcove

& on leaving the Inn
walk up Almaden
past the offshore banks
(the orchards burnt & dozed
when electronics came)

think of recent Santa Clara grads
hoping to retain the software concession,
steal the yup trade from Mountain View, fill the new
Civic Center with suits, music, beds of flowers, &
    sprinklers!

●

In the old day homes
these virgins were my mothers.
I was treated
as poor.

On the polished hardwood floor
rolling in play pants. In black habit
& stiff white coif
Thomasine bends to offer

penuché on a glass plate. Downstairs,
admitted to the work areas, the stone-floored kitchen,
Sr. Malachy supervising,
two Spanish women baking,

door open on a walled garden,
a red or yellow watering can, geraniums,
tall bending stalks of snapdragon.

Catherine remembers me asking questions.
'Is it all right?' 'No.' (My mother's voice.)
'Is it all wrong?' Nuns smiling. One eternal
moment the content of the other, as we sit,
talking.

# Raft

On the raft, floating down
whatever flows, Huck & Jim
close at the center,
one facing upstream, trying not to remember,
feels the pressure
of the other's shoulders, facing down

remembering
boardinghouses, communes, bars,
working in offices & mills,
weddings & funerals & wakes

sitting smoking behind a barn
(or was that a story?)
sitting in the bleachers at ball games,
riding in cars, once over a bumpy field
in Gordon's Buick

sex . . .
a lobster dinner . . .

I thought I knew those places.
They were the world, each one,
mountains beyond mountains, kingdoms,
wisdom & shining gold, territory,
& there was a mother, a lover, a future.

Now this raft goes faster & faster
& I hold in my mind a map
that is the map of the world

& at my back my other
watches the islands come swooping
past, & feels my back
warm against his, his precious one.

# Nanabush

That the world have no meaning,
no purpose, a top set in motion,

but that Nanabush be there, off & on,
a bird flying in your face,
to remind you

that is the meaning.

(Like the nun used to come
soundlessly up the aisle
& get you
            behind the ear
with her knuckle)

Is it really my job
to go through these files
(R. being on vacation),
if it won't lead me, permanently,
to a staircase to heaven?

Each of them looking back at you says
I am here for a lifetime, so are you,
& the new ones
                come on
                        while you
have time to think about it.

If you forget any of this,
I will time & time again remind you.
I will be shooting star, opening tulip

& also snowfall.

## Death Thing

I'm waiting for the bus
by the Safeway parking lot
(where George Little had his mill
in 1911, give or take a thousand years),

& I'm thinking about this death thing,
how it's outside any context
you can imagine, even one
it's self-identical with, the only item,

but how in thinking of it
we try to place it in a context
so it'll go away. Like the World Series.

     •

I'm waiting for the plane.
I'm halfway through the metal detector.
I can see the mountains,
a small plane landing,

hear Tom Mackay in the bar last night, joking:
'I have no fear of flying. Crashing, yes!'
Norma broke up. We all broke up, laughing dutifully,
in respect for his bravado.

     •

I'm in the Cloud Room, on the 11th floor
of the Hotel Camlin, asking my brother Gerald,

'Who did this to Seattle? Wiped out the street life,
the bars & greasy spoons on 1st Ave. & Pike
that fed Ft. Lewis soldiers in the Korean War
& us in the '60s?' He said, 'Committees.'

That grizzled vomit had to go.
They wanted a tasteful place to live their deaths.
They rebuilt quick, condos, afraid
those Ft. Lewis soldiers might come back,
climb up out of the excavations, snake past
the darkened construction fences, in the guise
of street kids. They did.

'It isn't even an intelligent game,' I said,
'but it's not a simple one either. It's politics,
keeping people in the dark, & like all games,
it runs out. Shit happens.'

                    •

I'm in a motel in San Francisco.
Leafing through a business magazine, I come across
an interview with an old high school buddy,
now sits on many boards.

'Sometimes,' Gordon says, 'I forget the motion
when the time comes to vote.'

                              Sometimes
I forget the motion, looking out the window,
thinking of contexts.

                    •

Hard to get my head around it,
no way to get my head around it,
my head's in it, I'm headed for it.

It'd be life I'd have to get
my head around, if anything.

'To learn that there is no Santa Claus
is perhaps the beginning of religion.'
Get your head around that, get real.

This context-bound reality you construct,
this facing up to death is just the fading
of the real sense of reality, fading
of the individual. We don't 'have to believe'
the world is for the young; it just is.

## The Set

Remembering how it felt
working on the *Grape*
in '72, doing layout
in a gray former grocery
on Powell — we'd take a break
at suppertime & head for the pub,
knock back six or eight draft,
a package or two of chips,
maybe a pickled sausage,
& tell the waiter,
'Take one for yourself.'

We were a part of history
in our mental spotlight, drinking beer
with trade unionists from the '30s,
in that battered pub (soon to be closed,
renovated & turned into a fern bar).
They told us tales
of struggles of the past.

We'd troop back, half-lit
through snowy darkness or summer shadow
to that gray, dingy, dimly-lit
former grocery, to finish our layout.
There was never enough liner
or blades for the X-Acto knives & the
typeset 'corrections' always came late
from the *Peak* & had to be pasted

in by hand, but the beer in our heads
kept us going past midnight — also the link
with the old union guys — with the dirty '30s —
we were for real — & we were dirty.

Do you miss all that? Do you miss the dirty '70s?
That sense there was a world & meaning
outside your mind? Tho skeptic Ed Dorn
said 'the set,' you could account
not just for the world but for nature itself:
the trees that leafed in the spring on Powell St.,
the stars — for you thought,
why would there be stars if there were
no world for them to shine on?

& by the third or fourth draft
your hangover would lift
& there'd be the sacred streets, in long
purple & orange stripes of sunset
to the eternal horizon,

& you called yourself a cadre,
a little yeast cell, making
tiny, correct changes in people's
consciousness, getting the paper out
on the streets. Miss all that?

I shot up to Rupert for no reason
like a steel ball in a Bally machine,
banging around the pink bumpers,
racking up points for god knows who or what.

I came almost to a stop, poised at the entrance
to one of those long, gently raked, steel alleys
you can roll down for years, decades, & still
be far from the flippers. Then I missed the world,
the beery romance of politics,
(the whiskey romance of poetry),
the set.

# The Berlin Wall

Why, now that it's breached, broken, does it cause
such consternation in me?

                CBC brings me
the cries of happy youth, the singing, people
climbing up on the now meaningless Wall,
drinking champagne —

                I see myself,
eighteen months ago at Checkpoint Charlie,
hurrying across the street to avoid
the grisly American museum —

                In the narrow corridor,
slipped my Canadian passport under glass to the unsmiling
visor-capped uniformed young official — he inserts a visa,
passes it back — a loud buzzer sounds, a door swings open
into the next holding-pen — exchange West marks for East
    marks,
another buzzer, another door — a block or so of speed
    bumps &
barriers to control cars —

                then on Friedrichstrasse I stand,
an official, legal visitor to the Deutsche Demokratische
    Republik,
approved museum-goer, café patron, *flâneur* . . .

The past is a prison I long for, the past is a holding-pen,
the past is eternity because I did not die then.
Now youth breaks out of Kreuzberg & Wedding, out of
    Pankow
on the east side (side no longer), flows unchecked
across the border, smashes the rest of the broken wall even,
to widen the space
                        & something in my old heart
wants to stop it, wants to retain
the orderly street, the fading State
offices, gilt-scrolled windows, resembling
banking rooms, that defined my ordinary
middle-aged eternity, my stroll, wants to
put the Wall back. As if time would stop,

as if when I went to Vancouver next week there might
be a Wall, a part of the city I could not enter except
by passing through the approved crossing-point (Broadway
    & Clark),
answering personal questions, giving bona fides of my
    existence, then emerging
on the far side, the good side, the dream side,
knowing myself to be a good citizen, inspected therefore
respected, & that the State (either of them) would protect me
from death.

If the young can be kept from knowing their power
(which is the power of time), if they can be made to accept
the reigning system, one memo, one regulation at a time,
with its bullshit rationale, then the old will not die.

Then the old will walk the streets of Vancouver & Berlin
fed by the respect that is paid to them by the State,

by the faces in their mirrors, & by the young, too,
unwitting collaborators, lured, conned, into the plan,

the plan behind all plans, the plan to control time.
We need not die (though we are very old), & you may remain
children, adult children. One more decade, one more year of
eternity . . .

But the reasons wear thin. Become disconnected
from the hours of the day. And the night. The places
where assent had been given are unattended.

A detour is found. The young see each other, not pictures
of the old. Then the Wall falls. One less memory is real, one
    patch of ground
liberated. And the old must learn that history

is not their house. They must learn, like the young,
to live by their wits.

## For Prince George

I'll listen to the news the day I die,
to hear who was elected, & if
the New Jersey Devils won the sixth game
of the Stanley Cup —
not because I care about these things
(truly I care less & less),
but the game is worth the candle,
lit by the candle.

At Christmas, when lovers' eyes meet over the candles,
their thought is not 'you,' it's pure meaning,
infinite horizon. I'd rather be a spectator.
I'd rather be a spectator than play games.
I'd like my mind to be dumb as a lover's.

Late at night the middle-aged play Monopoly.
One spills a drink. Slurred voices,
a peal of laughter. Like the old
balls & wreaths on the tree, that dully gleam
from the darkened living room, their thoughts
come out again, sure of welcome.

# Three Chinese Men

> The poet: one who constantly
> thinks of something else.
>
> *Czeslaw Milosz*

The three Chinese men, one with
Walkman earphones, passed by the window
of the Greek restaurant on Broadway —

no connection with the poet eating lamb chops,
facing away from the window, toward the bar,
where the owner kept appearing, a smile,
a hint of a question, on his broad face —
Is everything — is your drink — all right?

A fake marble fountain was gurgling,
a bouzouki tape played, the only other
people in the restaurant a young couple,
the girl Asian, the boy white, who seemed
to have just met & were talking softly but
continuously, as if fearful of shared silences —
A blind date? the poet thought, & then unaccountably
turned to look over his shoulder
out at whatever was there — air, wires,
buildings, a street (Broadway),
cars traveling at great speeds, & thought,
It's meaningless (as had become his wont
since attaining high office in the Party),

but looked a little longer,

& then, from his left, along the sidewalk,
conversing (well, two of them conversing,
the other had Walkman earphones),
three Chinese men. How could there be
men in a no-world? What was the one, the tall one,
saying to the other, & the third, slightly ahead,
what was he listening to? Beethoven?
Chinese opera? They passed by.

In all this nothing that surrounds you,
there was once something, there was mystery,
you didn't know what it was, it was all the more real
for your not knowing.

Then you got it down pat, you got it
fixed in your mind, you knew how to use it,
enter it. You went in & out of it, around the back,
first, where the discards were, then in the front door.
You were it, and it was you, too.

Then it began to disappear, as you will disappear,
poet, eating your Greek food. The owner
comes forward, still a bit hesitant.
'A little ouzo with your coffee, sir?'

## Spring '90

This is this spring. Mountains know no time.
Humans know time & say 'come round again.'
The snow, falling, fallen, knows no end.

Patches, melting, freezing, melting again,
have no thought of melting away, & the old
grass, newly exposed, is plain:
'I am neither old nor new, don't you see?'

If we could only see, we would never go.
Human time is tearing us away
from a time that if we turn back to it
at every moment says *stay*. This spring.

# A Sleepwalker

He is not alone when he dreams.
Only, when he perceives
a mistake in the dream-construction,
the others turn away,

& he is recalled
to that land he calls truth,
or death.

He makes no mistakes
in games. He acquires
magic symbols, is reincarnated
on higher boards,

& everyone who speaks,
he speaks,
rehearsing their voices.

None of them loves him
like the angels in the dream cities
until he notices
there are too many stars,

or the bicycle he is riding
in morning rushhour traffic
turns to money in his fingers
(folded twenties).

Sometimes in the middle of a phone call
he will know how it blends
with the files & the fettucine
into the skin of a dragon,

& sometimes a word comes close
to breaking the spell,
& he repeats, like a mantra,
'We are all here.'

# Mozart & Cold Cuts

(Flight 513, Vancouver-San Francisco,
1 June 1990)

Do you think
each day
is one less?

Does the sunlight
include a ray
of its absence?

Flying
to once 'home'
(Mozart & cold cuts)

Curved cabin,
blue ocean,
surf spatter,
brown hills —
reality
never answers.

San Francisco's
there —
cool, timeless,
like it was
before nostalgia.

Faint memory
of flushed boy-face
in 1950.
Running for judge.

Mary, born
1906, says,
'When I die'.
Bowl of pink pansies.

Orators:
on streetcorner, 'George
*Herbert* Bush ... ';
on traffic island,
'Homosexuals ... ';
on steps of Sproul Hall,
'If I had
30,000 ... '

Hard, the men
with blankets
& shopping carts.

In Jess's painting,
*Time Becomes Part of the Picture*
in the form of a fly.

Blake's fly
is a man
believing.

Here, in this blue
air, do you fear?

Here,
in this blue air,
do you fear?

Under the bay,
the train
speeding in the tube
rests on mud.

Would you give
the black man
(& the woman following
pushing the cart)
3 dollars & 20 cents
for bacon & eggs?

Why cry
for Matthew Broderick
in *Glory*
and not for them?

## Terrace Landscapes

### 1

The mares & colts near the college. The big single-family
houses built on sand & gravel, smooth rocks, once below
water. Did they want the smell, the farm smell? Some of
them might — might be glad — the farm smell connects them
to the earth — the earth has no purpose.

•

Fields as long as there is life, weeds sprouting from 'my'
land, quick after rain, from stony dirt. But not from the dirt
without stones — without so many — strange.

•

Breakfast with Pat & others — I float my idea out of Gould
& Bateson, that since evolution is blind it makes no difference
if my life seems pointless too — it is pointless — so, relax,
you're in tune with the universe. But I realize this is too
much for breakfast time — a negative Christmas present — &
if knowing there's no Santa Claus implies any responsibilities,
one of them sure is, no negative Christmas presents.

•

Standing at the bus stop, talking to Steven. Noticing the give
& take, conversation, life-activity. The bus comes. We get on,
ride downtown, pass the little farms, talk baseball, Canadian
culture. I always want to get my theories in.

•

Vancouver — being there — feeling marginalized — out of it. Stan's cracks about Terrace, & not just that but a feeling of being a hick or old-fashioned romantic, someone out of the '60s but not the hip '60s — out of Margaret Laurence world.

Stan & Scott hip to the new writing — narrative. Stan telling me, with a bit of an I-told-you-so voice, Bernstein is replacing Creeley (now retired) at Buffalo — only later do I realize this is a fact in the history of Buffalo — not art.

Disoriented — my idea of myself, as always, to be sharp, wiseguy — & desired — but now, now ageing, not interested in being sharp, smart — not interested — maybe because of the fear of addressing *any* content — that old, sad pseudo-project again — to hide somewhere — let nothing happen — then nothing will happen to me. Imagined to myself not saying a word about self, only answering if others asked, but being interested in *them* — well, I didn't have to be interested, they (Stan) were interested enough in themselves & I heard myself talking again about myself, my mingy facts, dull upcountry concerns, knowing every time I said the word 'Terrace' I was more out of it, marginal —

•

Terrace landscapes — landscapes of heart & mind — not just trees & clouds & straight streets looking south — a long mile — when dark all the 'Terrace-ness' goes out of it, there's just a dark space, a sense of trees & houses & a mile away, low down, lights of a street, gas station & neon of a hotel, as if that were the only street in the universe, all around flat land, then rising land, then mountains. Fog settling over, riding the flat of the airport hill — in the morning rising, restlessly

writhing upwards, from the river, & following the river, a
river of fog or mist atop the real river under.

The parking lot outside the Safeway is the centre, at night
a few cars still parked at the north edge, close to Lakelse,
maybe the glow of a cigarette visible, moving.

The imagination of the town fights with the imagination
of the land. The imagination of the land is creative, its
forms come out of the land, appear out of the hills, the
creeks between low hills, stride into the centre. Not Indian,
or animal — bear — nothing so specific. Maybe they are
geometric, Platonic — they are forms into which the people
and animals can fit their dreams.

The imagination of the town is imposed, a ruled pad. The
streets are the lines, they line us up. Driving we imagine we
are walking, the tree-lined streets (of Manawaka), on our way
to the stores, the bank or the credit union, the library, the
doctor. A dream of a town out of a primary reader.

City sophistication an added element. When you eat at Don
D, exotic foods served by neat boys and hippie ladies, you
can lose yourself in the world it creates — imagine Terrace a
community in harmony with other communities in a pacified
world — the places cornmeal & papaya come from.

More disconcerting, the last vestiges of the local — the Co-op
cafeteria — the oldest old men on canes in the sunlight. And
that reality isn't there either, disappears when you look back
to the Indians, back to the land. You realize you look back at
nothing. Again, there is nothing. It is all made up. Except
the forms.

•

Start at the same spot, near where I live, the 'horseshoe,' called that because the bench makes a horseshoe-shaped bend to the north around the flat land, once farm land, beneath it, extending south two miles to the river, which makes a nearly symmetrical bend to the south, enclosing the place called Terrace.

Across that plain cut the railroad & the highway, and from where I stand, looking a mile south to what the kids call 'Main Street' (Lakelse), there's a tiny cluster of lights, a floodlit gas station, neon bar of something else, a few white gleaming dots. Like it was the only street in the universe — not a very friendly universe either. A bureaucratic moon. Sometimes I think of Terrace as a spaceship. We're 15 light years out on our journey, all 15,000 of us — or maybe we're 75 years out. We've got a standardized Protestant society — malls, churches, schools, soccer leagues — & we don't know where we're going. Nor do we care. That seems an abstruse question. Are we going anywhere? Well, anyway, away from the Indians.

Away from the news.

Now there's snow on the landscape, on the land once farmed, now laid out in the rectangular blocks of an Ontario town (Leacock's Mariposa) on the north side of the tracks, & the same, but more straggly, on the south. When you get down towards the river there are still some farms.

•

I saw some posters in the CUPE office today, solidarity posters, one from South Africa, showing men & women with their fists raised & expressions of solidarity & determination on their faces. And I thought, these won't convince, any longer. People are turned off by posters with images of people on them. They remind them that they are people too.

•

Sparks Avenue — leads from my street (which is named after someone who lived here) down to 'Main Street.' It's an ordinary street — it has a sidewalk on the west side (except for the first block at the north end, where instead of a sidewalk there's a hardpan trail through the grass, between the storm ditch and the fenced-in yards. I walked down that trail this morning, on my way to the anti-poverty meeting. It wasn't hardpan, but slick with a little mud and wet snow on the grass quickly melting.

•

The bus broke down as we were making a corner in Mountainvista subdivision. The driver tried to cut it too sharp, the front wheels climbed up over about a foot of snowbank and then the back wheels didn't, there was a loud cracking sound as if the bus had run over a metal box. The driver turned off the ignition, opened the door, jumped down into the snow & disappeared. In a minute she was back, sat down in the driver's seat & got on the intercom. 'Are we stuck?' I said. 'I lost an air line,' she said. 'Can't move till that's fixed.' We were a quarter mile from the college.

Got out on the road, walking north. Heard a car coming behind me & stepped off to the side — a little too far, my boot started to sink down in the snow — I pulled back. The car gave me a wide berth.

It was the point in a storm, or a series of storms, when all motion ceases in the sky. The moon wasn't up yet, but there was still light in the sky, a dark greyish blue, some clouds in odd, wind-torn shapes, light coming up from the mill to the south, too, & the highway. Walking, just that quarter mile, alone, it was like I was back in Wyoming, hitchhiking, when I was a kid (26, but I was a kid), thankful it wasn't raining, there in the lonely dark but not sad to be alone, lone there, because I knew I was going somewhere, New York & even that was a way station, horizon beyond horizon, simply that I was young & it was all unknown & long ahead, that unknownness of life was better than safety, there was no concept of safety, there was, therefore, no concept even of being there, on the highway in Wyoming — I was just part of it, I was just *it*, in fact, no distinction. No distinctions needed to be made.

Ahead was life, that's all I knew. I heard a huge sound behind me, lit up like blazes a truck, cab & trailers came over the western hill & barrelled down at me, blowing its horn, the gust of wind off it almost knocking me down on the gravel shoulder. I walked on, into deeper night. The stars must have come out, I don't remember, or if it was cold, or even raining, though I think it wasn't raining.

I kept walking towards dawn. Cars kept passing me. I would whip around to jerk a thumb and maybe catch the eyes of the drivers, which was hard, because I was lugging a big, heavy suitcase. Around 8 a.m. a black convertible with California plates came over the rise, a single young guy, blond, sunglasses. I yelled, 'Hey, California!' He stopped ahead of me & I ran up & got in. A few miles down the road, doing about 70, we hit a dog, straight on. The driver didn't swerve, held the wheel steady. The rancher came out & accepted his apologies, said he knew we couldn't avoid it. That night the driver & I stayed in a motel near Omaha, separate rooms. I thought we should have slept together, but I didn't ask.

Terrace landscapes or any landscapes. A sound like a train or a plane or a truck. Wondering, for a moment, if life is simpler — oh no, yes, simpler — than I thought it was — are we back where the monk said we started, with the mountains, trees & sky? All the 'head trips' blown away?

Terrace landscapes — another engine sound. An oil-scape.

•

The dark. The fog moving across the field like a, like a. Nothing. Whitish nothing. Not moving. There. So many feet or metres up then sky & mountain beyond. Swirls at the bottom. Wet, dry. Follows the river, the river exhales, the damp turns visible, in cold, the breath comes from the warm throat — these things go on, these processes, giving, accepting. The trucks come from Vancouver with the meat & fruit & frozen dinners. The people float in the net, their minds go on & off, images of other people & places flash, wink, in their minds, against a picture they all agree is *this place*, earth, they live on top of, land.

Down below dark, out in the air at night, past the techno-lighting, dark. Distant sun, a whoosh of light & heat going past. The giant rock of earth, of home, between. Mirror moon.

•

The light shineth, & the darkness is forgotten. And what the light shines on? And how long does the light shine, before it goes out again, & the darkness returns?

Or is there any darkness? Only a world, our world, located on a planet, which we are subjecting to extraordinary stress — the air-borne & water-borne pollution — the noise — the vehicles — the money — the messages. The energy — all of this in light — but in darkness too, no one knows about it, no one sees it, only when the pressure gets to the setting when the light goes on, the problem presents itself — the snow, the war. It's dealt with, more or less, & then the light goes off, the billions of exchanges start up again, not in the dark (except at night), not even in the dark of the mind, but in a neutral space, indirect lighting, minimally furnished, a desk the centrepiece, the desk dark, polished, empty of any clutter — empty. A pure, rich, glossy, rectangular surface. And then the light goes out. No matter. It's time to sleep now. It's time to sleep every moment. Mama's little baby needs sleep. This is very close to the end.

•

Someone, say H. (This is the way it always starts — how else can it start?) It starts with H. H. is a person completely unknown, except that the colour of his skin is known (well, his gender is known), & the colour of his eyes, his waist-size, the shape of his ears — and then the way H. walks, that is not like anyone else walks, exactly, is it? When he wears a shirt & tie, on the job at Don D, his face can look as if poised on a column, etc. There are many things about H. that are known — many more that could be known — but the person, H., is not known.

Is the world H. lives in known? Is the world H. lives in the world H. knows? Ah, there's the rub. Imagine, if you want to, that the world we know H. to inhabit is the world H. knows he inhabits. The same world . . . located on a planet.

•

Terrace landscapes. Landscapes of the heart & mind — my heart & mind — mine only? Of the white heart & the Indian heart, a place intersecting with a scheme, a railroad, a mill to cut ties, & lay them. To connect Montreal with the other side

of the continent. Part of a larger scheme, to connect Moscow,
Berlin, Vienna, with the coasts, to build cities & ports &
launch steamships to connect ports across the oceans. This
clearing, this place on the river, meant for a purpose & when
the ties were laid men looking for other purposes to be
meant for (to be men for?), white men.

Indian purpose? Does it lead into the spirit world, does it
lead anywhere else but straight through your life to your
death & then into the spirit world & back through the womb
— with no merit gained or lost, no rising or falling on planes
of spiritual mist? There were Indians here, not right here
but near here, eyes in the dark, over the crags of the river
narrows, watching the whites blast rock & lay tracks.

•

Snow falling fast as if hurrying to get to ground because of so
much more to come — rough-edged *pieces* of snow, heaping
high over objects — cars & roofs & streets. Wind coming —
coming out of blackness, lifting the last fallen part, lifting &
chasing it, away, against the fence, over, over the snow-
covered street, into yards, up against doors, living-room
windows, & continuing, every time you look, out any
window, to hurry downward, gather, assemble, rise.
Then after it's fallen it has a finished look about it, as if that
was exactly the amount that had been intended. Now a
break. Stars come out, the top of the snow gets crusty. The
place now in a way possesses all this snow, like it possesses
all the Christmas presents that fill the aisles of the stores.

Kids make snow people. The snowman — a frightening being,
if he existed — not like Santa with a warm heart, a human
body, but something with no principle of form, heaped
together — someone — a being — with no principle
I like to see the snow melt, the sun come out, the heaps

decline, subside, the roof-shaped collections of snow on the roofs draw back from the edges, the paths in the snow get wider. The grader comes & pushes all the snow, now without even the form it had when it fell, form it stole from the forms underneath it, and would like to cover forever, pushes it up against itself

## 2

The real thing now — war.

All the lesser things sort of move back slightly out of focus & take their places in —

Our everyday concerns move back & are shelved — as in banker's boxes — they seem to have some kind of order — they are ready to come forward again — the most important in the first rank — the career plans, or life plans — the relationships — ready to come back into the present, the thoughtless space of everyday living, after this —

& the mind swims — Mulroney's rhetoric, calling on principles of humanity & enlightenment, quoting former prime ministers, doesn't convince but I can feel its power of conviction — Bush's speech less so because the quavery slippery person is heard through the voice as well — but Mulroney's is oratory — & I can feel myself wanting to believe, wanting to be one with him — the nation, the United Nations — humanity — & also with the men & women who are in our thoughts, in our hearts, there in Saudi Arabia & on the ships in the Gulf —

The message — to prefer *peace*, to work for peace, is to abandon *them*, the young men & women courageous, controlling their fear, ready to die

(& in Baghdad, people ready to die)

& in Saudi Arabia, the young woman soldier says, 'Don't worry, it's not as bad as you think at home, we'll all be home.' To stand for peace is to abandon their hopes for peace, & therefore we must stand for war if we want peace & peace if we want a worse war in the future & the mind reels, wavers.

•

And now, of course, we're back in Terrace, restored (that has a faint sense of put back in place, or put in storage).

We're back at the college, in the thick, in the thickets of discourses, prompted by the students, the techie discourse, the geopolitical, the petroleum, the ecology, what of the monsoons? I'm shifting, no, turning, from one to the other, to each person, with her questions, & all the discourses together make a fabric, a textile, something to wrap us in —

It isn't that the war has come home, or will come home, but that we have all been yanked (yeah, yanked) by our strings of media & money & need, by our need for sunlight & food & oil, back into the world, back into the realization (the 'reality') that we are all part of it, all connected. 'Only connect'? Only *reveal* the connections — hear how the skiers are protected, security, the Super Bowl (no electronic devices allowed), the smoke from the oil wells, the oil bubbling to the surface, no need to pump, no way to put it out. Sudan, Libya, Jordan, where is the perimeter?

'I want to die with my friends,' Irv Halperin said 25 years ago when SF State students asked him why he didn't return to

Israel. I want to die in San Francisco. I want to die in Terrace.
I want to die in a world that has time for my death.

•

We calm ourselves with language. The media calm us with
language. Behind that soft sound, reassuring vocables, fine-
tuning their positions, soft tech, blood.

No blood for oil. For the immortality all corporations know
as their right, that of the military-industrial complex.

•

Now the war drops out of consciousness, whole hours, half-
days, no thought of the war. Then it comes back. Is 'comes
back' the way you'd describe it? What happens is I *remember*
(did I forget? did I at some point say to myself, forget that
now?) Clear the field, for more important things, for the
freedom to arrange thoughts in your mind like pieces on a
board, but less strictly, the enjoyment is in coming upon
them, thinking them into life, against no background, the
infinite leisure of freedom. No war. Then it comes back, it's
like a fact, no image, behind it images crowd, the ones
from TV, or comic books — planes — the image — I don't
have TV, so for me it's a memory of a newsreel, B-29s over
Germany, or the South Pacific, in the closing years . . . there
would be more images but the censor — a circuit-breaker in
the mind — cuts out. It's like *remembering* you're going to die,
remember & as quickly forget — it's like arranging your life
so you have only that one thing to remember — and forget.

Peace — a glib term — absence of war — so there'll be nothing
to remind us — of man's inhumanity to man —
now celebrated. The word is out — the authority — the wimp,
Bush — grits his teeth & snarls his words — a soft accent — a

grimacing face — a smile that turns into a snarl — genteel — a
way to apologize, for not concealing, wholly, the ravening
face of power. No pretense it's anything but right makes
might makes right & peace is for priests with pious faces but
I am a tank I am a gun I am a plane. And the young hear —
his cagey, liney snarl is answered by their smooth,
thoughtless snarl. It's out, it's free, it's real, it's right.

Peace — a smarmy word — pointing to nothing but the
virtue of the one who offers it — cheap — I don't like reality
either but — 'People have to die, in war,' the girl interrupts.
What good would the peace movement do? What good is
peace? What good? Keep your head down & your mouth
shut & don't make the enemy think we're not all united
behind our troops. If you have nothing to say, say nothing.
What peace but peace of mind, & that we buy with — war.
Blood. That's why you have the right to have your peace
march. So be grateful for it. But get out of the way.

•

Winter 'hanging on' — so many 'knots' per hour, wind
at the airport — translates to so many km. Last night the
branches whipping, a sound like something tearing was
sudden dashing rain on the skylight. Later in bed, the wind
& branches sound reassuring, but why? It always has been.
Nature — just far enough away, but there, to say, I am here —
not evil — enclosing, decentering 'my' world, ironing out or
rinsing or blowing away fear & concerns — make even death
natural.

•

Read this morning Carl Rogers at 75 saying he had little fear
of death, no more apprehension than he would feel going
under anesthetic — and gave his version of Whitehead's

objective immortality, that what was of value in his life would continue in others' lives, & after hearing the wind & rain putting my fears in perspective that made sense.

●

Went from place to place today — the anti-poverty meeting, the doctor's office. In the waiting room noticed how many Indians are sick — watched a husky Indian boy playing on a toy where coloured blocks slide on curved rods, with a smaller blond boy. Saw the aggression starting in the bigger boy's face — male, but also mischievous Indian — get back at you — he will some day — try.

●

Reading Emily Dickinson in class. Things that happen make up a day. Rain & wind. 'A slant of light.' The rain starts & stops, the sun almost peeps through.

Before dawn, the melted snow froze over on the shallow puddles, fine, white, crazed cracks — step on them.

Here in class are twenty or so young people writing. In Arabia a war — the world. Peter said, 'I can only say one word — the world is *sad*.' Mentioning various students — 'He's a very good student.'

No purpose. We make up purposes, then we lie in bed terrified of the breaks opening up in the purposes we made — that we might fall. Rain & wind come, cover us with natural noise, the outside. Soon we quit shivering under the covers, fall asleep. There is no inside, no place where purposes & plans wait.

●

Or walking outside the Admin building for a breath of air,
the mist-grey world, think it's just the ordinary ageing,
more aware of contingency, of being a six-foot (slightly less)
organism walking on this earth that knows it's not the centre
of — no, scratch that — that no longer thinks it's essential to
any universe — even fictional. So extrapolating back 30-40
years, I can understand why my students read poems by just
glancing at the poem, taking it in all of a piece, & then
talking about their feelings. They believe in their feelings,
like I believe in the fog or the mountains.

•

The true colour of the landscape, the Terrace sky against
the Baghdad sky — another day of bombing while we slept
— or no — a day of cleaning up, salving wounds, surgical
operations — a *night* of bombing while we walk about in our
dazed world, people meanings can't quite get through to —

In the Learning Resource Centre this morning two clerks
talking about last night's movie, wondering *why* some
character had done something — as though it was real —

Also at lunch today, faculty & staff persons chatter of TV,
till someone, tangentially, says 'Saudi Arabia' (with reference
to a veiled woman, part of a half-hearted sexist joke) —

Look at the trees as if there weren't eyes, as if *no I*, having to
be either a complacent Canadian or some moral critic, the
egotism of any possible vision —

Look at the pools of melting snow, the 'lake' in front of
the college, fed by the streams & trickles from the black &
crumbly heaps, that flows, ever so slow, toward the Kalum.
Something reflecting in it, trees, people.

(Another article about the 'economy' that doesn't say it's
located on a planet (it's by Robert Reich, out of *Atlantic*),
distributed by management, tells us how 'education' (read
'training') fits into some supposedly predictable migration
of institutions, moving into the spreadsheet future, carrying
or dragging humans in their roles — visualised no doubt
(by management) as suspended in space surrounded by
healthful brisk yellow sunlight)

('It's just another committee meeting,' Joe Clark said, having
had stage fright before his first G-7 meeting, in Tokyo.)

I see a river of blood & garbage moving through a landscape
no less unreal than management's utopia — the mainstream, I
call it — big trees, rotting trunks, swamp water — & I have
pity on all of us spinning around in eddies or in stagnant
backwaters or with little rafts of idealism the marines or
coast guard keep beating back out of the channel, so the big
liners can pass —

The real sky behind the morning sky, the real air, an instant
behind the air we think we breathe, the real world ready to
pounce on the world we know, that once again eludes its
claw, but its reflexes are going

•

The McEachern decision. The faces of Natives, seen anew.
In the mall & the one or two in my classes who come shyly
in — when asked to read from Shakespeare they have soft,
almost inaudible voices, but they don't trip over words, or
race over them, like some of the white boys. I think of jet
planes bombing Iraq, tens of thousands of boys dead, like
those Hamlet imagines will die in Fortinbras's attack on a
'straw' of earth garrisoned by Poland, *which is not tomb
enough and continent / to hide the slain.* Today napalm

reported, the jellied gasoline shot from helicopter gunships, but in the *Sun* the letters say we should or should not approve according to whether we're pro-American or anti-American. Language slipping sidewise, to evade the point, any way, not to answer, respond, but to speak again, shift ground. The Natives are to blame, McEachern says, for not having grasped the opportunity, always there, to become part of the mainstream.

And where is the mainstream, is it the stream of 'goods' that flows from the mall to the house & garage, & from there to the dump? And how to grasp it?

•

Valleys. Looking from the air at snowdrifted mountaintops no one, no goat even, has set foot on, in niches the glaciers, in the valleys the crooked lines, like pen & ink, of streams, the grey curves of highway. Then encapsulated, riding, at a comfortable speed, home.

•

Look up close. Trees in a Margaret Avison poem

    *ragged on the windward sides . . .*
        *prepared*
   *for onslaught when the obliterating*
   *blasts sweep in again.*

Let the trees stop the words, let them stand in front of the 'decision,' immovable, at least not movable by language, bendable by wind, but returning to their growing space.

## 3

Geese in Frank's Field, black/brown/white: black necks,
brown wings, white chinstraps. I rode in a bus past the field,
I wanted to remember their colours, & the placement, & saw
the geese hunkered down in the field, in pools of melted
snow, sodden earth.

When the geese come 'home' or 'north,' we feel complimented,
start to smile on their return. Winter dies, willingly. Its last,
left, nothing is now but everything unnamed & surviving.
Lasting. Like the black necks, white-ringed (memory swoons),
brown-feathered, the blue, the white, the wet, the calm, the
oval, the ovary, the delta. Escaping. And all flowing away, the
incline, the trickle on that slight gradient of the cool seeping
from under the grey, cold, evaporating, upward, the skillful
pools, the turning. Bugs. Birds. Sodium. Let live. Shadow on
glassy, of the tall, bending, & then the blue again, & the
white scudding, & then the geese flying over & the sound,
undescribed. No feeling. No one to feel. The slight sound
of coughing.

There is such a wanting in all things whether one or many, to
be free, & whether part of a separate, & whether entangling
or loose. Untouched. Unknown.

•

Spring — a raven sat in the shrub outside my window —
heavy bird, bending the branch as it pulled with its beak at a
twig — the day before two ravens — then flew away, low over
the roofs of the big ranch houses to what's left of the bush,
trees & shrubs, under the bench — where do they nest?

•

What do we do? The snow goes, the many changes that are spring (don't list them) appear, & in that turmoil *we* — is there a *we*? I don't mean people, I know what we do as people, *down to an art* they say, Wittgenstein wanting macaroni & cheese because he had it yesterday — treat time like space, ride herd on vagrant thoughts ('that way lies . . .') & somehow take yourself off like armor, play naked, & deny deny deny at the mind's battlements. So we do this to do that to do naught. But that's our sickness, that's our daily tread, happy are we when our there is here — but that's not what life is up to. Oh, I know, sick feeling, to recognize again, life's up to no good, just up. The where we (yes, there's a we, we're all wee — stupid pun) are is not in my living room for instance, when I stand there I'm not there & if I were truly there I'd be a terror-shape. Like Snoopy trying to be like a tumbleweed, after a few tumbles he gets the point. Better to be intent, & call that a tent.

•

I thought the night before about a huge lament I wanted to make, how I could only express my feelings about the inevitability (which isn't even the right word, more the *certainty*, as Dr. Rank, in *A Doll House*, says) of death by a list, of all the things in life, tumbling over one another, like out of the Horn of Plenty or Santa's sack, one after the other, pleasures, visions, sky, spaghetti . . . let's face it, there's nothing you can say, or write, about that except that it's nonsense, it's going under . . . And yet it's the only thing you can write about, it's the only thing that stops language cold, up to its tricks, as always.

Language bounces off death & for a fraction of a second, at least that long, is stunned, & stays where it is (spaghetti for instance) before it bounces somewhere else.

Meanwhile the geese inhabit the field, with their eyes that see a mile ahead, unnoticed.

•

A little substance, solidity, comes to spring with these first after-supper hours when it's light. Not that tentative, pre-adolescent, that March tension. The 'braided' rivers, the channels making braids around the oval, tapering sandbars. The valleys were once filled with water, the glaciers extended. Now there's less ice, & less water too. That's odd — seems as if the glaciers melted, the rivers should rise, but they don't melt, they evaporate, & the rivers come from the snowpack, which comes from the ocean.

•

The boys with kerchiefs snapping their skateboards up on the dividers in the McDonald's parking lot, across from the bus stop.

# Moscow '91

In the hotel, marble staircase, marble walls.
Outside, the big stores, plate glass windows,
but abandoned, sad. The sign unlit.

But another kind of life is here, making deals,
business types (& gay men I'm sure), in twos & threes,
on the broken sidewalks, past the big, silent stores,
& in the parts of the landscaping that have gone back
to grass & trails, talk quietly —
it's like people reinhabiting their own ruins.

10:30 p.m. 17th floor window. A city. Not many lights,
but as far as I can see there are lights.

A loneliness, like that of a place for itself.

3:30 a.m. (dawn). Pale orange apartment blocks,
grey or purple mansarded roofs. Trees
along the streets & in the courtyards.
The university (with red star) floats on the horizon,
past the wide bend of the glassy river.

6:30 a.m. Walk to Kievskaya Station. Lots of informal
park space, for private life in public. People walking,
standing, sitting on park benches, thinking. There's more
freedom here than in North America. Freedom to be,
to sit on a park bench & think, to mind your own business.

4 p.m. The sadness — the city missing itself —
feeling the loss of itself — is the 20th century city.
Not the Czarist city of mansions & boulevards,
the Communist city. City of ample proportions, handsome,
designed by socialist architects & planners — city that speaks
of a new world, where people could live & walk in dignity —
in the *perekhody* (passages) connecting the metro lines,
in the stairwells of the metro stations, walls
unmarred by false images of human desire.

Kremlin. The icon makes eye contact.

They are the people I knew as a child —
their sense of themselves came from families,
grandparents, great aunts, aunts & uncles & cousins,
but also from schoolmates, teachers, nuns & priests,
& from reading, characters in novels,
& then most recently, characters in movies,
so their sense of themselves became more stylized,
but they were still diverse, as any human population,
until the consciousness industries began to work in
    consciousness as in clay,
to program minds with alluring images of preternatural
    perfection,
until everything else looked old & faded & boring,
all but this panicky search for a self one could own,

& I see them again on the steep escalator
in Kievskaya metro station, descending past me,
faces that reveal what we called
feelings or states of mind:
patience, humor, sexuality, vanity,
thought, spite, venom, self-satisfaction,
envy, worry, delight, happiness, love,

a quiet, contemplative look like that of the Virgin
in the Cathedral of the Dormition,
despondency, calculation, pride.

They are each in that moment
the being of the person, not something
she acquired in a transaction.
They arise out of countless encounters with other persons,
out of the *interanimation* of a human community,
as *life* — & they are not (yet) superseded by the power
of addicting unsatisfying dream images
because the walls of the spaces where they walk
are bare — the only images are the faces,
are *each other*.

& then the face of Oleg appears
in the silly cap & paper-doll livery
of McDonald's, handing me my *dva* Sprite,
gaping fecklessly, sightlessly, past me
into a disintegrating cosmos, a Soviet citizen
who at last does not know who he might be,
a receptacle.

The Egyptian cult of the dead.
The American cult of the living.

•

The football crowd. Hundreds & hundreds of young men, &
older men. One woman in a hundred, pouring into Sportivnaya
metro station. The round hats of young army & police bob
along in the crowd, not separate from, not policing it, but of it.
The chant goes up — *Soyuz, Soyuz* — for the team. The train
comes, all the doors open, the crowd piles in, together. In the
cars, the chant, intermittently, from one group, now another.

A young man holds a drunken friend, white-faced, about the
shoulders, tenderly. Apart from the chant, no talk. The mass
of men swings together in the speeding cars, then flows into
Kievskaya station. Up the escalator. Cool glass candles. The
chant. The boys, the men, together. No talk. The police &
army hats bob along. Together. No hint of violence. The
separate beings of all, for now, subsumed in the mass.

(But what if you were a Jew, or a homo?)

•

In Hunters Row
the skateboys glide.

The sadness
is of the *perekhody*.

## Union Hall

If the old are allowed to be young,
the young must consent to be old.

The actual time in Ireland must be
23rd century.
So far in the future to remove
the apparent present
into the deep past.

The flat façades & the shields of the breweries,
the housefronts painted the softest of hues,
yellow & blue, pink & redpurple,
but at dusk all Irish houses are grey.

The pub is a cell of joy,
honey-whiskey light & smoke,
& narrative hilarity,
& truly, no other life
's available.

# Cork

Can Cork offset its 'deceptively inconsequential air'
by twinning with Coventry, Rennes, San Francisco &
   Cologne?

# A Trip in Ireland

A poet among poets — one of the poets — with James & Jim,
Dennis O'Driscoll & Philip Casey. One of many poets — one
of all who are here — this one of all of us. No trepidation
here in Ireland (look that up). No fear of the moment, the
time (now) is safe in the past. Our deaths are after, not now.
This moment is always (& always) reclaimed by the symbolic,
by the falling of words into place (like dominoes?) — like
leaves. The words carry the urgency, shoulder it, it's their
own. The soul is relieved ('My burden is light'), & the body
lies down, laved in the *river of life*, with just the sense organs
protruding. Like a hippopotamus.

& what is lost, if everything is not compulsively decorated
(a boy just came to the door selling prints by Young Irish
Artists), but if the walls are left blank or a clutter of coins,
ribbon & train receipts on a tray, they casually fell too, like
leaves. Nature must not be kept out at all costs as in America.
A huge crack runs the height of the window like a stem.
Space left to rise like bread. Mr. Finegan is one of the New
Formalists.

So when I came here I felt sinking layer by layer — 'into the
bog,' one said, but it was only the companionable (Creeley's
word — Irish Creeley) — arrival at Inch — pint by pint —
Kavanagh knew — how not to die — breakfast after dark —
then to Rafferty's.

Walked around Dublin Zoo — clockwise — the animals
watched me, & were quick with their tricks — the giraffe with

those knobs, the cheetah posing (no strap), bears acting
Canadian, i.e., feral, like Americans back from the wild, like
Robert Bly's neo-men. 'The time of men is gone,' James
proclaims, in — what was that bar? — and, 'sit down, I'll get
it,' & later, musing, 'The ham was fine.'

& the train took me, rackety-rackety, to Cork, as the elegant
Killarney woman seduced, verbally, the young North
Carolina golf pro: 'How many members have you in your
club?' 'It's just a public links.' (Look that up.)

Time doesn't all run one way. Time, too, has a geography,
has caves, & you can climb down into time using only your
naked toes & fingers & carry a small light bulb in a wire
cage on a string around your neck, & that is sex, explosive as
Miss Universe thighs or the angel in Waterstone's with the
knapsack that pulled his t-shirt sleeve high on the right
shoulder & his lazy rope of gold curls as he moved from
Fiction to Psychology — I could not lift my eyes — I remember
thinking, he's too big for me — too big for all the dark-haired,
short, wide-faced ageing sweating youths — & their sisters —
& the odd priest with leather satchel, running to catch — &
my cousin crossed himself as he neared crossings, & crossed
himself as, it seems, he thought of hate or injustice —
liturgical —

all the tiny bottles, the cordials, & Cadbury's biscuits

'Will you have the last pint with me?' And the angel moved
in & out of consciousness, still ungraspable

# Arklow

The stunned faces — the stalled lives

A battle no one knows is going on (on 'our' side) —
no one cares to fight. The pub a nursery,
here lessons in intricacy. But they sing Paul Simon
songs instead of the old
uprising, insurrection. Here a priest died.

Their furniture will save them. The carved & polished
& inlaid interiors of the nursery. Whispers behind
whispers. 'They'll look you straight in the face
& never say a word. In Wicklow. In Wexford
people are friendlier. They'll start up a conversation
with you.' Soccer its own world.

McDonald's no more invasive than Coca-Cola logos
melt in the cuban syntax, crammed & cluttered windows
& then a big, bare space. Light falling across the faces,
made for the occasion. The boy telling the man,
agitated; the man listens, arms folded, his right
hand to his chin, pensive. All history stops here,
unfolds, for a moment, its medicine chest.

Homosexuality, vegetarianism, green politics. We are
living in the dawn of the old girls' world.

9 p.m. Boys kip, men skip.

# Coolgreany

To be or not find
motives or interests,
exchanging parts of a story,
some days back, in this 'very' room,
in this house that was part

(& the earth, & all the houses
of parliament, lines drawn crooked
or straight, to demarcate
property, are not re-drawn
again & again, as the universe jigs
from no-being to being

(as the symbolic order
re-flowers in the brain
when a good sleep follows
on a day wasted trying to think
in images)

but they continue,
trees fall in the forest
& you find them later,
true to your disbelief.

You are trying to climb
a sliding cliff, a giving way,
to what you glimpsed through multiple
shifting screens of your own devising

(all of this talk), some real event
that will refract

If being is only taking arms against
phantoms, then suffer, fortune,
& switch on, switch off, mind,
knowing now no world's really there
but something Platonic & personless

Here's a human reality,
unmistakable — a mouth,
eyes that emit light,
a pulse, a history

# The Void

Love it or leave it.

*New Poems 1992-94*

# London

I saw Canary Wharf & Stonehenge too,
& no one knew what either one was for.
What posturings beneath the trilithons
hallowed the cooling gore.

What schemes the thousand vacant windows frame
of avarice, beyond the cheated strand,
no traveler need detain who feels the tap
of the uncastellating wave on sand.

Who warily, from pub, hotelward wends,
cutting across the lampless square between,
crouches in fear of rovers that contend
the precious pavement of the scene.

'The economy' is a weapon at the throat
unconstrained by how you vote.

# The End of Bohemia?

*for Liam O'Connor*

When Julian Maclaren-Ross sat down alone
in London's Wheatsheaf & asked, Where has everyone gone?
he knew the answer was they'd all gone home,
some to earth, some to Paddington. Finally, it was time.

And when Jack Spicer had to shout to be heard
over the goddamn jukebox, Gino's began to fill up
with the kinds of people he'd warned about in his poems,
police agents, *Chronicle* reporters with beards
    on the soles of their feet.

(In Vancouver we only had pub night on Tuesdays.
Nevertheless the management of the Cecil
tried to drive us out, first with country music,
which failed, then with strippers, which succeeded.)

And as you tell it, Liam,
after Paddy Kavanagh died,
some of the old ones held quick consultations
with their doctors, but the young ones
held dinner parties, & gave over attending
McDaid's entirely. (Not to mention UCD
    being moved to the suburbs.)

(But maybe Post-Modernism itself is just a phase,
prelude to an era (as Jameson suggests)
of neo-proletarian uprisings. Then, in the truces,
what colours might Bohemia wear?

## Upper Fraser Canyon

The railbed
was blasted out
of the mountain,

& the rock
is held in place
by rusty straps,

& you can see
where you came from
through the tracks.

The canyon.
And its beauty.

## The Puck

skids — skitters. Sometimes it rolls,
then it's harder to whack in. The attackers
cross the blueline. Pass — to the point — he shoots!
Players pile up in the crease. The goaltender
sprawls — whistle. Where's the puck?

Face-off, in the defenders' zone. The two players
edge forward, sticks descend. The linesman
slams it down. It's back in play.
(The puck must always be in play.)

Draw back, to the stands, the thousands of fans.
One is saying, 'Watch the puck.' The other,
'Watch Bure, it'll come to him.'

Draw back further, through the TV cameras, the cable,
out in the tube, a dazzle of pixels, the game,
in the living room — the curtains slightly drawn,
spring evening entering. Watch the puck —
start to tell a story, ask a question,
change the subject, & EYYYYYY — they score!

Bure or Linden or Ronning, arms raised in triumph,
flies into his teammates' embrace.

Second period. Light a joint. Now watch the puck
for dear life. The puck is life, like a word.
The huge surrounding fucked reality. Sense of

your body, hunched, & the doomed city.
Ah, but there on the screen, white knights, Canucks!
You know them, know their names, know
the rules, sophisticate, obedient as they.

Then a commercial, cars or beer,
& all about the *cliffs of fall* (not Ronning).
You remember yourself & forget the puck.
You are like Prometheus on the rock,
you can't fall. The car drives into your head
& is wedged there. The TV set with a car for a head,
the pterodactyl, is eating you.

Third period. Now the beer is heavy in your head
& the dope keeps calling you back
to your damned self. Nonetheless you know
what you must do, keep your eye on that black blur

or miss the pass.

# Virtual Reality
### (Broadway & Macdonald)

*for Andy Klingner*

Another umbrella bumps by me in the rain
touching off a murderous rage. This is *another*,
not the Other I learned to love in graduate school,
but some asshole (from the suburbs) casually entering

my space. Excuse me, he says, but not politely,
more as if he thought me an imbecile, who didn't know
this was a public street, I am in his way.
Furious, I jerk on, start to cross Macdonald,
& now brakes screech, & a new voice yells, 'Asshole!'

& I think, 'Fuck you.' The light was with me
when I stepped off the curb — or was it?
(I was thinking about that asshole with the umbrella.)

But safe on the other side I delete all this
& reenter the familiar idyllic despair
of *my* world, my virtual reality.

## Amor

'Hop on my bike & head out
to the Luv-a-Cup
in Port Moody,

smile on my face,
condom in my pocket
& 2 bucks for a latte.'

## Another Monastery

*for Jay & Pete*

Here are the cups & bowls,
here are the packets of food,
& the fruit bowl, replete
with apples, bananas & grapes.

Here are the fetish objects
of the absent abbot:
hubcaps hung on the wall,
teeth of radiator grille,
& rubber dinosaurs that make
the house plants loom gigantic.

And here are the young monks,
working at jobs in the world,
& living in common by rules
unknowable, either to them
or to the old fox.

## Voice Mail

The phone has mutated. They have managed
to keep it from ringing. It was always
the worst thing, to have in your ear
a reconstituted voice, telling its story,
so like yours. You'd have to take that caller
on a trip you knew led nowhere
just to keep from knowing
it was you, also, calling. So you stilled it,
& now when they dial they don't get
you anymore, they just get
instructions. And no one there to know
it's your self, trying to reach you.
'I want to speak to a human being.'
That's you, the human being, calling,
& as long as you don't have to listen
to that, you can get on with your work.

(I called California, & heard
voice mail in Spanish.)

## After John Newlove

I'm approaching it from the wrong direction, & so I don't
recognize it. Someone — that's as basic as you can get —
someone is who we are. Someone arrived, just a moment
ago, from the previous moment, where not-he, not-she, had
spent a century, an eternity, but then not-his, not-her, lease
was up, & someone had to skedaddle — & arrived here, not
knowing what it was not-she, not-he, confronted, was over
against, because not-he, not-she, approached it from the
wrong direction.

If this is the world, then where am I,
what is this loneliness, this outpost?
Or if I am not I, but only someone,
then there is nothing I am over against.

Finally we all face this together,
but don't know what it is, even
though no longer approaching it, in the heart
of it, in our hearts, but still, somehow,
from the wrong direction.

From someone's heart.

## The City

I don't want to walk on Granville Mall     walk past the
children     hear their eyes read my thoughts
They crouch in entryway     squat or sit     legs skinny
unfed     shaved head & tattoo, pierced flesh

Suits go by, briskly     The children
read their thoughts     or vacant privacy     (heads turn,
eyes lowered, fingers meticulously roll a smoke)

Voices corroded, raspy     worn by the effort of denying
despair, just for a word or two     the words muttered,
laconic     (like signals)     spoken when needed
for practical reasons     (except when the demon of rage
breaks free)     Is it     not to let
the mortal breath catch the contagion of
analysis?     If you found yourself
saying something that took too long to say, using a
conjunction, say, *unless, but, nevertheless* —
cut the crap!     unless     unless you had to
get past the sour facts
                                        as if a suit,
or a nice middle-class lady bent down &
extended her hand for you to place your foot
on — the first step — up — & say all the
nice words — *unless, it wouldn't have, if only,*
*I never*
          It's not those words we live
by, but the unspeakable ones — maybe they can be

kept true by shouting them, like the
ultimate, *not!*
                    They read your thoughts —
how can you live, only caring about money?
how can you live, not caring about caring?
how can you walk by, carefree, thinking
about cars, jewelry,
your mutual funds, security?

The orthodox say:
*Human nature is a mind that grows in a baby's brain,*
*& learns to compete*
(As these children's bodies are starved)
                *compete compute consume*
(As they huddle together, you stand apart)
                *compute*
(As they seek to be friends & overcome bad feelings,
you seek to overcome weakness & be secret enemies
of all you smile on)
                *compete compute consume*

*& learns skills, like*
*friendliness, courtesy*
*& different languages*
*for different games*

By the towers the children sit, naked
By the towers, with black stick legs,
torn cloth, tiny holes in the mesh

The towers rise     of steel & glass
up over the streets     in the carpeted suites
the shadowless light     the fine, filtered air
cleansed of static     the molecules, polished

the suits stride back & forth    & get paid
for their faces    their eyes
are information receptors    cut of a jacket,
knotted tie    sweat drops    'synchilla sweaters
made of recycled Coke bottles'

the hand is an information receptor
(the hand is a starfish, the information enters
via the mouth)

*You have to have more than five senses*
*to keep ahead of the world — up here*

*I have a profit-maximizing module*
*implanted in my hindbrain, it*
*overrides family values.* The data
is sorted, screened    the little things
fall through the screen    finer & finer
screens    the little things fall    the trays
are emptied    into the clouds

*I have the finest of minds — compete, compute*

High above the children with their stick legs
red spots of anger, white faces

new towers rise, cranes ratchet up their sides

at the top, a visual racket

# The Aanme

*for Peter Weber (1940-1994)*

Peter, I see you in your office,
your desk covered with student papers,
documents, communiqués, reports,
& your own memos & lecture notes
off your portable — I could always tell
it was a memo from you by the typeface,
elite, & the single spacing,
& in the memo read your voice, animated,
interpolating apposite data (or jokes about Hitler)
in mid-phrase
                        you were gunning for the henchmen
of capital, in whatever guise —
employers' council, task force on human resources
(that weasel word liberals gagged back
as if there were no difference
between a human being and oil, or a computer)

but if queasy liberals questioned
historical fact, you'd be quick to remind them
human beings can be requisitioned, used,
used up: the corvée, the gulag

& with your hands deep in the clay
of a student's mind, make him say it:
'How did they get them to work in the camps?'
'For food, right!' A smile,

a blinder in the way
of knowledge of power     falls

You taught history as a humanity,
though the historian be a scientist
rummaging in the archives

(Bismarck Hitler Stalin the true experimental-
ists — heads of research centres
(not quite your words
but I think your thought)

               Poli Sci?
'Like teaching English' (a smile
for the English teacher)

Economics — now that was something else —
you attacked the board — neoclassical
curves swooping, the chalk snapping —
to display its sterility
in a single graph —
               Say's law
(& marginal this & that) confuted
by Keynes: the point of equilibrium
is not full employment, but total indifference
to human need (the kids open-mouthed, blank-faced,
or sniggering in the back rows)

Philosophy? 'Sophisticated escapism'
from life — history — at the time of
the Gulf War: 'I have only one word —
the world is *sad*'

*quantillâ prudentiâ*
*orbis regatur*

•

Look up from behind that crowded desk —
a smile of equality, fraternity,
conspiracy (my job —
to get the students to the meeting)

We made you our leader
because you would not play
sectarian games —
'I know *who* I am, not what I am'

You needed to come to terms
with the people running things —
cooperate, & yet, oppose
the satraps of the petty principalities —
Terrace, Kitimat, Prince Rupert —

for education —
for 'working people, Native people & women'
(& maybe One Big Union)

so Don Anderson called you Machiavellian
& you responded, politely,
'Machiavelli has been misunderstood.'

•

Daniel's image, not mine:
'Who is that *teenager*?'
Frame spare as the bike's,
yellow hair flying, sweat shirt & jeans,
whizzing down the airport hill

(mine: pedaling to Kleanza in the rain,
seen from the inbound bus)

•

The state papers of great powers
after war or revolution
are sealed for a generation
(to sanitize reputations).

So you could sit in the backyard in August,
read books, drink beer,
never catch up. In 'this little place,
where nothing will ever happen.'
Except your death.

'I'm going to die,' you said.
And looked      the distance.
And still had a smile for life, for us.

        'The *aanme*,
the personal animating essence
inside the breath. The *aanme* continues
to interact with the living after
an individual dies, and becomes
an ancestor'
(Mayan)

*druk*, friend

# Poem Enclosing Its Dedications

& now I'm looking at someone
in a t-shirt, who comes out of the shade
of his apartment & wags his fingers, briefly,
against the steel frame of his glass door
so they flash white, in the sun.

The sun makes the apartment building opposite
reflect the light, off its paint,
dirt-streaked.

Two trolley poles skim past (the top halves).
The wires sway
        for Judith Copithorne & Daniel Ignas
The hemlocks or firs or whatever move slightly
in the breeze
        for Renee Rodin

Another man in a t-shirt gets out of a grey car
(I don't know the names of things —
trees, makes of cars).
The blue sky says nothing,
but what would you expect it to say —
do you think that behind it there are wheels?

A man with a yellow shirt & a
yellow cap. A blue truck. If I don't know
him by name why should I know the truck's
family?
        for Barbara Munk

A lyric poem.
A man in a brown vest & a t-shirt
carrying a plastic Safeway bag.
The traffic signal sways.
                           The blue sky means the sun
is warming Vancouver.
                           Another bus,
this one going west, to Dunbar or UBC,
so I can see the full length of the poles.

Maroon car. Man in blue jeans & grey
sweatshirt & black helmet on a bike. Another
guy on a bike. Woman with raspberry red coat
walks up old concrete steps with a Safeway
bag.
     Red car.
Cherry red. Wild cherry.

Four people, one pushing a bike.
Green sweat, white helmet.

Man sits at desk, looks out window at
cream-coloured apartment building, parked cars,
conifers he doesn't know the name of, only
knows they're conifers cause he can remember them
greenblack in winter — at trolley wires &
thicker black (hydro?) cable, sometimes birds
sit on, crows, pigeons —

old '20s 2-storey gable-roofed house on
Trafalgar, Avalon milk truck, blue
sign of Westside Ski & pink sign of
Montri's restaurant

& blue sky all behind this. Sky blue.
Sits writing poem. Wowowow of ambulance.
Stops.
　　　Stops writing. Poem goes on, world goes on.

# The Young Monks
## Understand Eternity Better

The young monks understand eternity better,
playing with their dogs, repairing their bikes.
For them sunlight is sun, not a phenomenon,
& rain rain —
     they seem to have bodies
between their minds & the outside world,

while for the old fox the rain starts
in his heart, as it did for Verlaine,
& he feels responsible that it rains on the city as well.

Brightness of brightness   the young monks sing
like O'Rahilly   the old Cork poet

& though the rain on the city can make it rain in their hearts,
it never works the other way, as it does for the fox
for whom the rain starts in his heart . . . (etc.)

And when the sun shines,
brightness of brightness sing they
like the old Cork poet O'Rahilly

(but the fox remembers the Corkery history
that the brightness is of a dream, a legend, a vision,
& he sings, contingency of contingency,
knowing the sunlight to be insubstantial,

a visitation      of energy
of the universe      an accidental, phantom universe
that is in fact no more than is signified
by the words *sunlight & universe*
in the philosophy of Wittgenstein, Rorty, et al.


& that having deprived the world thus of any reality
we put language on a pedestal, a plinth . . .


Well, if the Sun were to walk into my room & address me,
sure I'd believe in him, I'd be a young monk myself
for whom language is trash, like yesterday's *Province*
with the lies from Bosnia & the true sports scores,
lies & truth together, indistinguishable,
put out in the blue box to be recycled
(though the city is rumored to deliver them secretly
to the landfill, there being no market
for mixed (& indiscriminate) lies & truth —
until the old trees are cut down, killed,
        to make toilet paper
& forms for pouring concrete for the skyscrapers
        of Kuala Lumpur
                        all which the young monks
dismiss, disdain, it has no reality
compared to the brightness
        & warmth of sun breaking      through shriveling
        rainclouds, & coming into the kitchen!


The young monks ride their mountainbikes
        & rollerblade
& ski
        in a world forever unnamed, or
        rather one that eludes naming, as
miracle upon miracle it reveals itself

(I'm not saying the young monks have no feelings,
no doubts, no fears, no dark night of the soul —
only that their unnamed bodies keep their
    minds from intruding
on the palace of the sun, the rollerdrome of the stars

# NOTES

**Gentle Northern Summer** *500-mile-long smudge*: There was no smudge; the cars returning from the coal port were sprayed with a fixative. *Vivian*: Vivian Pederson, long time resident of the Bulkley Valley.

**Terrace '87** *Dudley Little*: Millowner and MLA, son of George Little, 'founder of Terrace.' *Sam Clark*: Title character in Frederick Philip Grove's 1944 novel, *The Master of the Mill*.

**San Francisco's Gone** (Part 1) *COP*: College of the Pacific. (Part 6) *Bean*: Walton Bean, California historian.

**Nanabush** See *The Rez Sisters*, by Tomson Highway.

**Death Thing** *George Little*: See above. Santa Claus quote from Gregory Bateson, *Angels Fear*.

**The Set** *Grape*: Vancouver 'underground' newspaper, 1972-73. *Peak*: Simon Fraser University newspaper.

**Cork** The quote is from the Cork Jr. Chamber of Commerce.

**The End of Bohemia?** *UCD*: University College, Dublin

**The Puck** *Cliffs of fall*: See G.M. Hopkins, 'No worst, there is none.' Ronning's first name is Cliff.

**The Aanme** Latin quote: 'With how little wisdom the world is governed.' (Axel Oxenstierna)

# ACKNOWLEDGMENTS

Some of these poems were previously published in: *Arc* (Ottawa), *Blue Canary* (Milwaukee, WI), *Four Realities* (The Caitlin Press, Prince George, 1992), *Giants Play Well in the Drizzle* (Brooklyn, NY), *Line* (Simon Fraser University), *Mirage #4 Period(ical)* (San Francisco), *New Directions* (Vancouver), *North Coast Collection* (Prince Rupert), *Northwest Passages* (Northwest Community College), *Northwest Sketches* (Terrace), *Pembroke Magazine* (Pembroke State University, NC), *Points North* (Prince George), *Sodomite Invasion Review* (Vancouver), *The Capilano Review* (Capilano College), *The Vancouver Sun*, *The Worm in the Rain* (Larkspur, CA), *Vancouver Review*, *Witness to Wilderness* (Arsenal Pulp Press, Vancouver, 1994).

An earlier version of 'Gentle Northern Summer' was included in *Opening Day* (Oolichan Books, Lantzville, BC, 1983).

George Stanley was born in San Francisco in 1934. He moved to Canada in 1971, and now lives in Vancouver. His previous books are *Opening Day* (1983) and *You* (1973).